British Design
2003

Interior, Retail
and Event
Design

Interior, Retail and Event Design

BIS Publishers

British Design 2003

British Design 2003 consists of three volumes:
-Branding, Graphic and New Media Design
-Interior, Retail and Event Design
-Product and Packaging Design

This multi-volume survey of British Design is published
by BIS Publishers in association with The British
Design Initiative, www.britishdesign.co.uk.

BIS

BIS Publishers
Herengracht 370-372
1016 CH Amsterdam
T + 31 (0)20 524 75 60
F + 31 (0)20 524 75 57
E bis@bispublishers.nl
www.bispublishers.nl

Any overview of British design is only as good as the work that it showcases. *British Design 2003* is the first survey of its kind, offering a cross-section of the most talented design agencies in every sector. Compiled in the first half of 2002, a period in which the industry was recovering from a less-than-soft landing following years of growth, it reflects the determination of British designers to show their creativity, perhaps precisely because the market has been slow. Each of the almost one hundred studios presented here has contributed in its own way to the striking impact of the survey.

In enterprise, creativity is the key to success. Everything else is about keeping the wheels of the business turning. The best entrepreneurs must have the courage and vision to harness creativity, and the ability to choose partners from a wide range of studios and consultancies. Creativity is essential in defining branding strategy, in devising visual identities to accentuate recognition and product knowledge, or helping brands come alive on Internet. It is a vital part of getting products and product improvements into new markets, and equally important in transforming interiors or retail spaces by implementing a corporate identity strategy.

This first British showcase of recent work by designers in every discipline, makes the search for the ideal design partner a bit easier. *British Design 2003* provides an instant impression of each studio's work – an essential reference tool for whenever professional creative input is needed. Judge for yourself: there's creativity here to suit every taste.

Rudolf van Wezel, Publisher, BIS Publishers

"In the last decade design has established itself in the strategy of most businesses as an activity brining tangible benefits. Design brings competitive advantage to the marketplace, whether in product development, communications or environments, our task in promoting these benefits becomes easier year on year as our function is integrated into the corporate culture." *David Dalziel, Creative Director, Dalziel and Pow Design Consultants*

"Design the appropriate application of creativity and innovation. Style the personal application of creativity and innovation. Taste is a matter of opinion". *Ian Caulder, Creative Director, Caulder Moore*

"In an increasingly overcrowded and competitive visual environment, looking different from others is becoming more difficult. Yet still designers manage to come up with original solutions which stand out from the crowd." *Chris Ludlow, Senior Partner, Henrion Ludlow Schmidt*

"Ultimately the industry needs people who are imaginative with content – designers that understand its value and have the talent to manipulate it, enhance it and deliver it in an engaging way for the recipient." *Gordon Druce, New Media Director, Subliminal*

"One of my biggest bugbears is the over-reliance on research that clients have. They research projects to death. In my view, the more the project is researched the more likely it is to die a death." *Satkar Gidda, Marketing and Sales Director, Siebert Head*

"Behind every good piece of design there needs to be a great idea". *Peter Widdup, Director, River Design*

"After more than thirty years in this business I have come to realise that design as a tool for communicating will only have truly come of age when clients no longer see it as a separate activity to the rest of their business. Design is not a camouflage, hiding poor service delivery or product design, nor is it a mirror, reflecting every line and wrinkle. The designer creates a portrait of a company – it can be a little flattering but it must above all be truthful otherwise the consumer simply won't recognise the face."
John Furneaux, Furneaux Stewart, Design Director

"British design, in its recent manifestation of say the last twenty years or so, is concept led. The idea is greater than the manufacturing process generally although sometimes that process is the idea". *Paul Daly, Director, Paul Daly Studio*

Contents

Interior, Retail and Event Design

51% Studios	... 2
ACQ Architects	... 4
AD Creative Consultants Ltd	... 6
BDP Design	... 8
Blair	... 10
Carte Blanche	... 12
Caulder Moore	... 14
Checkland Kindleysides	... 16
Communication by Design	... 18
Conran Design Group	... 20
Corporate Edge	... 22
Corsie Naysmith I.D.C	... 24
Dalziel & Pow	... 26
Design LSM	... 28
DJPA Partnership	... 30
Fern Green	... 32
Furneaux Stewart Design & Comm.	... 34
Helen Yardley	... 36
Imagination	... 38
JudgeGill	... 42
Jump	... 44
Oakwood dc	... 46
Path Design	... 48
Paul Daly Design Studio Ltd	... 50
Powell-Tuck Associates	... 52
Rawfish Design Consultants	... 54
Redjacket	... 56
Shopkit Designs Ltd	... 58
Studio Hagger	... 60
Two by Two Consultants Ltd	... 62
Warner Associates	... 64
Zynk Design Consultants	... 66

Advertisements   ... xv
Call for entries   ... xxi
Addresses   ... xxiii

Interior, Retail and Event Design

51% studios Architects

Management: Peter Thomas, Catherine du Toit, Geoffrey Makstutis
Staff: 5
Founded: 1995
Memberships: RIBA

1-5 Clerkenwell Road
London EC1M 5PA
t: +44 (0) 20 7251 6963/f: +44 (0) 20 7251 6964
email: info@51pct.com
51pct.com

Formed in 1995, this is a multi-disciplinary practice whose projects, theoretical and realised, span architecture, industrial design and furniture, landscape and urban strategy. Studio members are engaged in publications, exhibitions and digital technology.

One of the practice's largest projects is a £7.5m centre for the arts in Cornwall, where it took its design cue from the existing courtyard of an old farm and created a hierarchy of protected and connected courtyards, ideal in the extreme landscape of Bodmin Moor. A granite and glass 'crystal court' at the centre of the scheme provides a winter garden and performance space. Recent projects include offices and a showroom for P W communications 1 + 2 in Clerkenwell, London and video-editing facilities for Cut + Run in Soho, London.

Designing with light is a practice trademark. For P W Communications, housed in a former loading bay, a bright ambience with dimmable, full spectrum lighting is synced with employee monitor cycles to prevent headaches. The fish tank is at once an animated 'rest centre' for screen fatigued eyes and a light filled filter to the street.

51% studios has worked on a diverse range of architectural projects, each managed to a high creative standard. The practice's perception of what can be achieved in response to a brief is highly imaginative. An example is 'designing in' the use of reflected sunlight.

This level of detailed thinking is evident throughout the practice's work. Idiosyncratic features range from the inversion of a traditional staircase in the rebuilding of a house in Dartmouth Park, North London 3 + 4, to the 'warm minimalism' of a Victorian house in Chiswick, west London.

A responsive interest in the possibilities of existing buildings, and a readiness to think long-term, including environmentally, are key aspects of the firm's ethos. 51% specialises in treating each client individually.

pw communications, ziggurat building, saffron hill, ec1

1

the greenhouse, dartmouth park conservation area, nw5

3

acq Architects

4

Management: Avery Agnelli, Hal Currey, Kim Quazi
Contacts: Hal Currey
Staff: 5
Founded: 1999
Memberships: ARB, RIBA

26 Mortimer Street
London W1N 7RA
t: +44 (0)20 7436 4866/f: +44 (0)20 7636 3396
email: info@acq-architects.com
www.acq-architects.com

acq is a young practice with a growing reputation.
acq's experience ranges from large architectural
projects to retail concepts and stores as well as office
refurbishments.
A series of office interiors completed by acq radically
rethinks the relationship between work and leisure.
Whatever the budget or scale of a project acq applies
the same vigorous creative process, coupling design
practicalities with a sustainable approach.

Recent clients have included
Channel 4 Television
Channel 5 Television
New Media Spark
Sunley Holdings
Bodas
Refuge
Clickmango
Marakon Associates
LVMH Holdings
Adcore Strategy

1. Concept design for relaunch of Pucci Stores LVMH Holdings
Paris
July 2000
2. Concept design for Stella McCartney Stores
Stella McCartney London
December 2001
3. 24 Hour Bar and Entertainment Space
Channel 4 Television London
January 2000
4. Reception Island and Boardroom
Marakon Associates London
July 1999
5. Store for Bodas Bodywear
Bodas London
October 2001

AD Creative Consultants Ltd
design consultants

Management: brian mathews (managing), john graham (creative)
Contacts: john graham, susan sanders
Staff: 6
Founded: 1974
Memberships: design council

the royal victoria patriotic building:
studio 17/18 trinity road
london
london sw18 3sx
t: +44 (0)20 8870 8743/f: +44 (0)20 8877 1151
email: mail@adcreative.co.uk
www.adcreative.co.uk

We provide design solutions that are tailored to any individual client's requirements, we operate no house style and pride ourselves on unique solutions.

Clients
Alizé International
Broadreach Group
Compass Group
Cork International
Dixons Stores Group
Elizabeth Arden
Gallaher Ltd
GiGi Expresso Bars
Henkel Arabia
J. Wray & Nephew (UK) Ltd
Marks & Spencer
Sainsbury

1-2. Beauty department, Marks & Spencer
3. White Box, Marks & Spencer
4. Wine department, Marks & Spencer
5-6. Currys wayfinding and segmentation, Dixons Stores Group
7. Taste Sandwich Bars, Compass Group
8. The Link identity and store environments, Dixons Stores Group

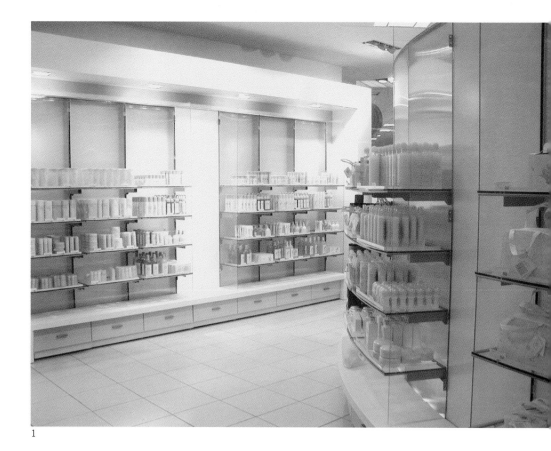

1

2

3

BDP Design

Management: Martin Cook
Contacts: Martin Cook
Staff: 46
Founded: 1972
Memberships: Chartered Society of Designers,
Royal Society of Arts

16 Gresse Street
London W1A 4WD
t: +44 (0)20 7462 8000/f: +44 (0)20 7462 6349
email: m-cook@bdp.co.uk
www.bdpdesign.co.uk

BDP Design are a multi-discipline design group with
expertise in all aspects of design in the public and
private sector. Our experience spans retail, leisure,
education, workplace and transport design.

Our strength lies in the overlap of a wide range of
creative disciplines enabling us to provide creative
solutions across a diverse range of projects. We have
worked with many leading brands on projects both in
the UK and throughout Europe.

We are an integral part of the BDP group, who are
recognised as Europe's leading team of architects,
designers and engineers.

*See also volume Branding, Graphic and
New Media Design p. 8*

1. NikeTown, London
2, 6. New workspace solution for BT, Mayfair, London
3. Brunel University, Uxbridge
4, 5. Glasgow Science Centre
7. e-play concept for Rank Leisure

Management: Bill Lanisek, Rob Edwards, Neil Elliot
Contacts: Bill Lanisek, Rob Edwards
Staff: 9
Founded: 2001

12 St James's Square
London SW1Y 4RB
t: +44 (0)20 7849 5510/f: +44 (0)20 7849 5520
email: contact@blairinc.co.uk
www.blairinc.co.uk

We are a design consultancy specialising in the
creation and execution of exhibitions for corporate
clients attending trade shows and brand owners
requiring representation at public exhibitions.

The heart of our proposition for business, is the
belief that exhibitions are a combination of two critical
elements - the creative and the tactical.

In creative, we consider those aspects of a successful
exhibition that ensure the appropriate application
of design and its impact on fulfilment, as much as
those aesthetic attributes that can mean so much to
highlighting competitive advantage.

Turning the concept into reality and fulfilling the
promise made by a creative proposal is where our
expertise in the management of project detail shines.
This awareness allows us to blend seamlessly the
many elements inherent in effective tactical fulfilment.

We are passionate about design and believe we can
best serve client requirement by presenting the most
relevant and innovative solutions possible, for us this is
a key element in establishing a sustained relationship
with clients.

We are also an innovative organisation in the way
we seek to manage the relationship between project
information and partners throughout the project
lifecycle; we do this by including project partners in
the earliest stages of dialogue.

Our belief in mutuality and the transparent sharing of
information means barriers to fulfilment are removed,
resulting in a more productive and efficient experience.
Whether client, agent or third party supplier, we are all
project partners sharing a mutual desire for the right
result.

See also volume Branding, Graphic and
New Media Design p. 10

Blair Inc Ltd
12 St James's Square
London SW1Y 4RB

t +44 (0)20 7849 5510
f +44 (0)20 7849 5520
e contact@blairinc.co.uk
w www.blairinc.co.uk

blair design exhibitions

4-5 Fitzroy Mews
London W1T 6DG
t: +44 (0)20 7387 1333/f: +44 (0) 20 7387 9333
email: info@carteblanche.co.uk
www.carteblanche.co.uk

Company profile
Carte Blanche is a London based international
consultancy specialising in the design and architecture
of retail, leisure and office environments. We have
exceptional working relationships with our clients
because we understand the psychology of brand and
space and how to deliver abstract and complex
projects on time and on budget. We have won
numerous awards for our work and we are recognised
by industry peers as innovative thinkers and reliable
implementers.

Awards
Topshop Store of the Year - Retail Week '99
Whittard T-zone Retail Environments - SEN '99
Topshop Theatre in Retail - SEN '99
Debenhams Leeds Store of the Year -
Drapers Record '99
British Museum Small Shops & Single Stores -
Retail Interiors '01
British Museum Retail Environment - Design Week '01

1. - OFFICE   Offices for Rocket, Creative Media Consultancy,
London, UK. The Think Tank: Bringing individuality and
inspiring creativity in the work place.
2. - LEISURE   Champneys City Point, London, UK. Health,
Beauty and Fitness. Creating a modern and relaxing
environment for the luxury brand.
3. - RETAIL   British Museum, London, UK. Grenville Shop.
A seamless transition from Museum gallery to Museum shop.
Customers believe they are buying an original ancient artefact.
4. - RETAIL   Allders Department Stores. Perfumery. Strong
branding, simple clear presentation, compelling visual impact.
5. - RETAIL   Whittard of Chelsea, Tea and Coffee Merchants.
t-zone, London, UK. An emporium selling the sensory
experiences of tea; taste, smell, texture, colour, enjoyment,
experiment.
6. - LEISURE   Springhealth, UK. Health and Fitness Clubs.
Changing colours and music through the day makes your health
and fitness environment suit your mood.
7. - BRANDING & LEISURE   Reviva, UK. Health Clubs for
Women. A new, refreshing brand name that reflects the needs
of modern city-centre women.

where retail
meets leisure

5

6

Caulder Moore
Strategy, Branding, Interiors, Graphics, Design Management

Management: Ian Caulder, Irene Maguire and Terry Moore
Staff: 20
Founded: 1990
Memberships: D&AD, DBA, British Design Initiative, Chartered Society of Designers

The Coach House
273A Sandycombe Road
Kew
London TW9 3LU
t: +44 (0)20 8332 0393/f: +44 (0)20 8332 1195
email: info@caulder-mooredesign.com
www.caulder-moore.com

Caulder Moore is a leading international creative consultancy whose key objective is to effect a tangible commercial impact on our clients business. Our team includes skilled specialists in interior design, graphic branding, architects and project managers.

We posses a recognised skill in interpreting the values and ethos of each of our clients into creative, highly successful and memorable design solutions.

Our reputation is based on over 10 years of creating new concepts and revitalising existing brands for a range of internationally known brand names. Our clients come to us for ideas, fresh thinking, inspiration and effective impactive solutions.

Awards

D&AD - Silver Nomination
DBA - Design Effectiveness Award
SEN - Creativity in Retail Award
Marketing - Best Use of Design in Retail & Distribution Marketing
FX - International Interior Design Awards - Best Independent Store Showroom
Retailer's Retailer Awards - Best Design Award - Nomination

Clients

Aquascutum, Asda, Charles Tyrwhitt, Christian Lacroix, Clarks, Coast, Escada, Giulio, Guess, Hackett, iBlues, Jo Malone, K Shoes, Mappin & Webb, Margaret Howell, N Peal, Scotch House , The White Company, Warehouse, Whistles, Value Retail, V&A Enterprises

Caffé Nero, Charles Worthington, Chez Gerard, City Centre Restaurants, Coutts & Co, Daniel Galvin, Eldridge Pope, Greene King, Inventive Leisure, Le Meridien, Luminar Leisure, Parisa, Po Na Na, Six Continents, Spirit Group/Punch.

1. BRB, Harrogate, UK
2. The White Company, London, UK
3. Giulio, Cambridge, UK

Our investment in store design has helped to deliver exclusive access to key designer labels and the privilege of numerous awards. The success of our stores has been exceptional. Caulder Moore have enabled me to realise my vision.

Giulio Cinque

Checkland Kindleysides

Management: David Checkland, Jeff Kindleysides
Contacts: Jeff Kindleysides, Adam Devey Smith
Staff: 110
Founded: 1979

Charnwood Edge
Cossington
Leicester LE7 4UZ
t: +44 (0)116 2644 700/f: +44 (0)116 2644 701
email: marketing@checkind.com
www.checkind.com

Checkland Kindleysides specialises in design for consumer experience and communication. We take an holistic approach to our work ensuring consistent delivery of message and maximisation of the commercial effectiveness of each project. We work internationally, offering a complete project management service in collaboration with our network of global partners.

Expertise
Retail & Interiors
Graphics & Point of Sale
Brand & Corporate Identity
Web & Multimedia
Exhibition Design

Clients Include:
Levi's
Rolls-Royce Motor Cars
Bentley Motors
Boots
Manchester United
Mothercare
Speedo
Vodafone
Royal Doulton
Ray-Ban
Lunn Poly
Nautica
Amtico
Hush Puppies

Recent Awards
Design Effectiveness Award 2000
Retail & Leisure Category - Levi's London Project

Retail Week Award 2001
Store Design of the Year
Lunn Poly Holiday Superstore

ISP/VM&SD - International Store Interior Design
Competition 2000/2001
Lunn Poly Holiday Superstore
Levi's, Seattle
Speedo - Special Award for Fixtures

Retail Interiors Awards 2000
Retail Exteriors - Levi's Flagship Store, San Francisco
Out of Town Stores - Lunn Poly Holiday Superstore

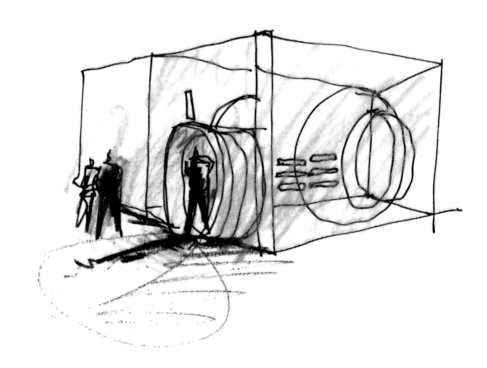

DBA Design
Effectiveness Awards
Retail & Leisure
Winner

Retail Week
Store Design of the Year
Winner

ISP/VM&SD
International Store
Design Competition
Winner

Retail Interiors Awards
Out of Town Stores
Retail Exteriors
Winner

Levi's San Francisco Flagship

Levi's Berlin Flagship Customise Area

Levi's London Flagship

Cinch - Levi's London Icon Store

Speedo Flagship Covent Garden

Cash Desk

Basement Changing Rooms

Speedo Juice Bar Identity

Mothercare Out of Town Format

Graphic Navigation with Emotive
Photography

Café Area

Cash Desk

Lunn Poly Holiday Superstore

Superstore Entrance

Superstore Interior

Lunn Poly 'City' Format

Bentley Marque Identity

Bentley Showroom Berlin

Bentley Retail Environment

Showroom Interior Berlin

CHECKLAND KINDLEYSIDES : DESIGN CONSULTANTS

Communication by Design
Design Consultancy

Management: Geoff Aldridge, MCSD
Contacts: Patricia Sinclair
Staff: 8
Founded: 1978
Memberships: Design Business Association, Museum and Exhibition Design Group

6 The Courthouse
38 Kingsland Road
London E2 8DD
t: +44 (0)20 7729 4000/f: +44 (0)20 7739 5728
email: info@cbdint.com
www.cbdint.com

Communication by Design is a highly successful, independent design consultancy. We specialise in the design and build of both permanent and temporary exhibitions, interiors, road shows and other special events.

Since starting in 1978, we have won a number of awards and built up a global reputation for innovation and excellence. We have also developed many long-term relationships with our clients of which we are very proud. Although totally dedicated and highly professional, we also believe that work should be fun!

We offer our clients a full design and project management service, from initial brief through to final build. These skills are supported by other in-house capabilities including graphic design, research and copywriting. Perhaps somewhat unusually, we can also provide strategic communications consultancy, and business, science and technology interpretation. Time and again, these skills have proved invaluable in helping us to understand our clients' products, service and business requirements, enabling us to deliver commercially successful solutions.

Over the years, we have naturally built up relationships with other complementary specialists in fields such as architecture, lighting design, interactive displays, audiovisual and multi-media.

We have a broad client base and extensive experience of most major exhibition venues throughout the world.

Clients
BBC Worldwide
BG Group
Blenheim Palace
Carlton International
Celador International
FremantleMedia
Granada International
Hallmark Cards
Hozelock
Lloyd's Register
ON Digital
Pilkington plc
Ragdoll
Sanyo
V&A Museum

BBC Showcase, Brighton

Granada International, MIP TV, Cannes

Pilkington, Technology Centre, UK

ON Digital, Ideal Homes, London

Lloyd's Register, Posidonia, Athens

V&A Museum, London

Exhibitions | Brand Experience | Museums | Visitor Centres | Interiors | Signage | Literature

90/98 Goswell Road
London EC1V 7DF
t: +44 (0)20 7566 4566/f: +44 (0)20 7566 4555
email: peers.detrense@conrandesigngroup.com
www.conrandesigngroup.com

Conran Design Group was founded by Sir Terence
Conran in 1956. In over 40 years there are few
retailers, industries or services with whom we have
not worked. We have a rich history, particularly in the
world of retail design, and one which we are proud to
draw upon. This wealth of experience enables us to
take a sanguine, long term view of trends, economies
and events as well as exploiting the short term oppor-
tunities that arise in the marketplace. We have local
knowledge and a global perspective which allows us to
handle international projects whilst embracing specific
cultural needs.

Clients
Airbus Industrie
Albert Heijn
Austin Reed
Body Shop
Boots
British Airports Authority
British Airways
Byte
The Co-Operative Group
Diesel
Do-it-all
Foschini
Habitat
Hammerson plc
Laura Ashley
L'Oreal
Max Factor
McLaren International
Oasis
Oxfam
Sainsbury's
Sears
Shell International

1

2

6

8

9

1. Spread for Trevi premium shower brochure
2. Cover for Diesel design and build manual
3. Spread for BT Ignite business to business brochure
4. Cash desk design for Deisel
5. Carrier bag for Avenue fashion store, Cyprus
6. MFI furniture flagship store
7. Café, Albert Hiejn xl store, Arnhem
8. MFI furniture flagship store, appliance display
9. DieselStyleLab store, London
10. Avenue fashion store, Cyprus
11. Britsh Council/Design Council Millennium Products travelling
exhibition, Europe, Far East & South America
12. Cookshop, Albert Heijn xl store, Arnhem

4

5

11

12

Corporate Edge

Management: Chris Wood, Ian Sherman
Contact: Peter Shaw
Staff: 130
Founded: 1997
Memberships: D&AD, DBA, CIM

149 Hammersmith Road
London W14 0QL
t: +44 (0)20 7855 5775/f: +44 (0)20 7855 5850
email: p.shaw@corporateedge.com
www.corporateedge.com

Corporate Edge is the UK's largest independent branding and design consultancy, formed in 1997 through a merger of two of the UK's pioneering marketing services companies: brand consultancy CLK and design consultancy Michael Peters Ltd. Offering a unique breadth and depth of branding and design skills Corporate Edge works in all sectors creating and evolving product, service and corporate brands - our skills include futures, research, strategy, naming, design, corporate literature, new media, interiors and architecture.

With a portfolio of over 60 clubs and spas in the UK and Europe, Corporate Edge Interiors and Architecture have established themselves over the past 15 years as one of the leading health and fitness design teams.

Clients
Anchor
BBC
BG Group
COI
Cadbury Schweppes
Calcot Manor
Cannons Group plc
Champneys
Clubhaus
Ericsson
Gist
GlaxoSmithKline
GUS
Guinness
ICI
Inland Revenue
Nestlé
Pearson
Reed Elsevier
Shell
Stax Leisure
Tesco
UDV
Wagamama
Williams F1
The Work Foundation

See also volume Branding, Graphic and New Media Design p. 14
See also volume Product and Packaging Design p. 34

1. Photos clockwise from top left; Champneys Citypoint, London. The Harbour Club, London. The Amida Club, Beckenham; - Pool, Changing room & Spa.

Corporate Edge

INNOVATIVE AND CREATIVE DESIGN AND ARCHITECTURE FOR HEALTH FITNESS WELLNESS AND SPAS

Corsie Naysmith International Design Consultants

Management: Ken Corsie, Stuart Naysmith
Contacts: Ken Corsie, Stuart Naysmith
Staff: 20
Founded: 1995
Memberships: IDI, BDI, CSD

Threeways House:
40-44 Clipstone Street
London W1P 7EA
t: +44 (0)20 7436 8505/f: +44 (0)20 7436 2133
email: k.corsie@corsie-naysmith.co.uk

Corsie Naysmith is a London-based, award-winning, international retail design consultancy that boasts amongst its clients some of the most prestigious new generation retailers and brands.

Seeing our role as problem solvers, with a core objective to increase sales of the client's products or services, the team's approach is both innovative and stimulating.

We work integrally as a part of our client's team from the product and retail brand outwards.

Our goal remains consistent throughout to ensure that our design solutions are in-line with our client's commercial and aspirational objectives, delivered on time and within budget anywhere in the world.

Clients
Harrods
Jelmoli
Sokos
La Rinascente
Roches Stores
Eircell
KPN Telecom
UPC
HMV
Adidas
Foot Locker
Gruppo Coin
O'Niell
Street One
Sehm
Sogaro
Alldays
Asda
CICS
Gruppo Finiper
Iper
Vitrashop
Wella
Alpha Retail
Jil Sander
Gucci
Giorgio Armani

1-2. Menswear designer collections - phases 1&2, Harrods, 1999-01

FOOD & BEVERAGE

FASHION /
ACCESSORIES

DEPARTMENT STORES

CORSIE NAYSMITH
INTERNATIONAL DESIGN CONSULTANTS

fresco

RETAIL
DEVELOPMENT

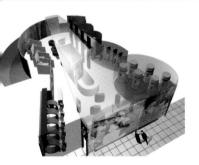

COMMUNICATIONS
& MEDIA

BRAND MANAGEMENT

Dalziel and Pow Design Consultants

Management: David Dalziel, Rosalyn Scott, Jackie Ware
Contacts: David Dalziel, Rosalyn Scott
Staff: 33
Founded: 1983

5-8 Hardwick Street
London EC1R 4RG
t: +44 (0)20 7837 7117/f: +44 (0)20 7837 7137
email: info@dalziel-pow.co.uk
www.dalziel-pow.co.uk

Dalziel and Pow, established since 1983, have developed a reputation founded on effective design solutions for retailers in Europe.

Through understanding clients' brands, concepts are designed to influence the market and achieve a dynamic environment through interior, branding, packaging, art direction and new media services.

River Island and Tottenham Hotspur's Spurs Store concepts have both been awarded industry merits.

Client list
Ajax, Netherlands
Arnotts, Ireland
BRE Multibank, Poland
Boyers, Ireland
Ethel Austin
Glasgow Rangers F.C.
Great Universal Stores
Guinness UDV
Hallmark
House of Fraser
Hugo Boss
Jaeger
John Lewis
Jones Bootmaker
Laura Ashley
Lyle & Scott
Nokia
Penneys
Primark
River Island
Signet Group
Tottenham Hotspur
USC
World Duty Free Europe

ENVIRONMENTS

01. Hugo Boss, showroom and store, brand consistency across all channels
02. Spurs Store, the Tottenham Hotspur megastore at White Hart Lane
03. John Lewis, perfumery, accessories and menswear for this established department store chain
04. Primark, brand environments and packaging, bringing quality to the value sector
05. Jones Bootmaker, rejuvenation of this footwear branded retailer
06. River Island, nationwide, a benchmark fashion multiple

BRANDING PACKAGING NEW MEDIA

DALZIEL + POW

APPLYING OUR **CREATIVITY, KNOWLEDGE** AND **INTEGRITY**, WE DELIVER CONSISTENTLY SUCCESSFUL DESIGN SOLUTIONS. WE STRIVE FOR EXCELLENCE, BUILDING PROFITABLE BUSINESS PARTNERSHIPS, WHICH EXCEED OUR CLIENTS EXPECTATIONS

ALL-**AROUND**-DESIGN
European Design Agency Association

Dalziel and Pow are members of All-Around-Design, an association bringing together independent design consultancies throughout Europe to further develop the presence of design. Existing and potential clients benefit from increased knowledge, resource and creativity from each member with the ability to receive a personalised service in any one country

Design LSM

Management: S. LaBouchardiere, S. McCarthy, P. Southgate
Contacts: Rima Shuman
Staff: 15
Founded: 1988

The Bath House
58 Livingstone Road
East Sussex
Hove BN3 3WL
t: +44 (0)1273 820033/f: +44 (0)1273 820058
email: mail@designlsm.com
www.designlsm.com

COMPANY PROFILE

Our fully integrated design, architecture and turnkey
capabilities provide clients with a variety of
comprehensive services that combine creativity,
knowledge and commitment. By understanding
current market influences and the importance of a
fresh, open-minded perspective, Design LSM provides
the most effective solution.

CLIENTS

Accor Group
Calthorpe Estates
Carluccio's
Gruppo
Henry J. Bean's Plc
Hilton
Lacoste
Ladbroke Casinos
Le Meridien
Pied a Terre
Spur
St George
The Macdonald Hotel Group
Universities and Student Unions
Voodoo Lounge
Whitbread Plc

DJPA Partnership

Management: Marc ten Bruggen Cate,
Hans Muysson, Arthur Brandenburg
Contacts: Jonathan Gibson (UK), Robert Kuiper (NL)
Staff: 60
Founded: 1989
Memberships: DBA

Unit i4:
22-24 Torrington Place
London WC1E 7HF
t: +44 (0)20 7470 6700/f: +44 (0)20 7470 6701
email: jonathan.gibson@djpa.com
www.djpa.com

Lemelerbergweg 31A
Amsterdam 1101 AH
PO Box: 12935
Amsterdam 1100 AX
t: +31 (0)20 79 888 88/f: +31 (0)20 79 888 89
email: robert.kuiper@djpa.com
www.djpa.com

Profile
- DJPA Partnership is a leading European design
consultancy with 60 staff, group sales of £7.7m in
2001 and offices in London and Amsterdam.
- We offer clients a range of specialist design services -
packaging, retail, graphics and multimedia design.

Clients
Allied Domecq
Auping
Gentiluomo
Grolsch
Konmar
Nestle Purina Petcare
Novartis
SCA Hygiene
Shell
Sony Europe
Unilever Bestfoods

Our vision
Our vision is to create new horizons for our clients,
their brands and ourselves.

Brand World
We believe that leading brands succeed in creating a
powerful, single-minded visual world to express what
they stand for and apply this consistently across all
areas of brand design. We call this Brand World and it
is at the heart of everything we do.

Our strengths
Our specialist design skills, our multicultural staff and
our understanding and experience of many different
markets within Europe allow us to see the big picture
and take on any design challenge.

See also volume Product and Packaging Design p. 40

1. Auping, Pan European Shop in Shop
2. Via, Dutch Food Retailing
3. Sony Center, Pan European Franchise
4. Fashion Cafe, Dutch Interiors

Fern Green

Management: David Fern and Nigel Green
Contacts: David Fern
Staff: 6

email: studio@ferngreen.com
www.ferngreen.com

profile

Fern Green has been in practice since 1989 and has established an international reputation for the creation and implementation of a diverse range of contemporary environments. These include shops, offices, health and beauty services, post-production suites and exhibitions.

Each project is directed by an understanding of individual client requirements and aspirations. We work closely with our clients to ensure that the designs are functional, appropriate and accessible.

Our aim is to create environments which help to establish individuality, enhance a business operationally and improve personal motivation production and well being.

clients

Blanco (Spain)
Body Shop
Boots The Chemists
Boots Opticians
Clerical Medical
Dentistry 100
The Cocteau Twins
Earth Centre
Ecco Shoes (Denmark)
Kookai
Michiko Koshino
The Natural History Museum
Relax
Red or Dead
Sir Alfred McAlpine
TBI plc
Tesco
Welsh Slate
Workspace Group plc

1. A space.
2. Relax, Massage & Juice Bar - Soho, London.
3. Ecco Shoes - UK & San Francisco.
4. Dentistry 100 - City, London.

Furneaux Stewart Design & Communications

Management: John Furneaux, Laurie Stewart, Nick Matthews, Nick Swallow, Ray Hole, Adrian Little, Julie Barnard
Contacts: Caroline Buchanan
Staff: 35
Founded: 1991
Memberships: British Design Initiative, Chartered Society of Designers, Design Business Association, Museums Association, Royal Institute of British Architects, Themed Entertainment Association

London Office
16E Portland Road
London W11 4LA
t: +44 (0)20 7792 9000/f: +44 (0)20 7792 9270
email: caroline.buchanan@furneaux-stewart.com
www.furneaux-stewart.com

American Office
Detroit
751 Chestnut Road, Suite 205
Birmingham
48009 Michigan
United States
t: +1 (248) 593-9411/f: +1 (248) 593-9412
email: julie.barnard@fsdetroit.com

Company profile

A clear focus upon both the message and its intended audience characterises Furneaux Stewart's approach, whether in its award-winning work for clients such as English Heritage or in its Bentley and Volkswagen pavilions at VW Group's ambitious 'brandland' at Wolfsburg in Germany. The company's portfolio encompasses exhibitions, interpretation, graphics, live events, new media and architecture. In all its projects, a successful fusion of different design skills can be traced, with one common aim: clear, compelling communication.

Clients

186k
The Acropolis Museum
British Waterways
Cardiff County Council
Commonwealth Institute
English Heritage
Heritage Lottery Fund
National Trust
OSRAM
Rolls-Royce & Bentley Motor Cars
Skoda
Snowdonia National Park
Volkswagen AG

1. The authenticity, power, heritage and craftsmanship of one of the world's most sought-after automotive icons is brought to life for Rolls-Royce & Bentley Motors at the Frankfurt Motorshow.

2. 'Life in a bag': an exhibition focusing on the contents of people's bags over the past fifty years and the role of Vaseline as a classic handbag standby.

3, 4. An FX Award Winner, the Volkswagen Pavilion at Autostadt is solid yet transparent, a shimmering 18m sphere inside a cube of glass. Inside the sphere, a 360˚ film translates Volkswagen's 'Spirit of Evolution' into human terms.

5. Avebury Manor Barn, a visitor centre that brings to life the mysteries of the Neolithic World and tells the story of the people who discovered, investigated, recorded and excavated this 6,000-year-old site.

6. The Bentley Pavilion at VW Autostadt. A 13m spiral - the power vortex - descending into the main body of the building.

7. GAIA, The Centre of Ecology, an exhibition for the Goulandris Natural History Museum which presents a balanced view of the global challenges facing the planet in an entertaining and accessible way.

1.

2.

3.

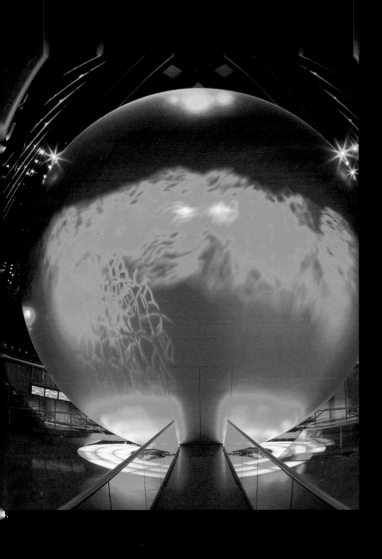

Helen Yardley

Contacts: *Louise Flesh, Nancy Edwards*
Staff: *9*
Founded: *1983*

A - Z Studios:
3 - 5 Hardwidge Street
Bermondsey
London SE1 3SY
t: +44 (0)20 7403 7114/f: +44 (0)20 7403 8906
email: info@helenyardley.com
www.helenyardley.com

Helen Yardley's studio was established in 1983 and
has become synonymous with excellence in design and
quality. The studio designs and produces area rugs,
carpets and textiles for walls. We work to commission
and also produce a collection of standard designs. Our
aim is to create something that is functional, works
visually but is capable of carrying layers of meaning
and therefore able to transcend simple surface
decoration.

Clients:

Bank Slavski, Warsaw, Denton, Corker & Marshall
British Ambassador's Residence, Moscow, Ahrends,
Burton & Koralek
Citibank, Brussels, IDEA
Clarence Hotel, Dublin, United Designers
Dresdner Kleinwort Benson, London, BDG McColl
Eli Lilly, Surrey, Arup Associates
Institute of Electrical Engineers, London, Lee Fitzgerald
Architects
Portcullis House, House of Commons, London, Michael
Hopkins & Partners
Basil Spence House, Beaulieu, John Pardey Architects

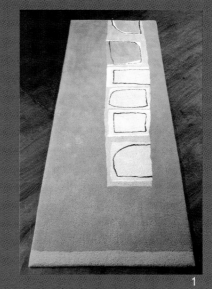

1

2

1. Hop Skip salsa 80 x 245 cm
2. Millenium 180 x 280 cm
3. Triptych marmalade 170 x 275 cm
4. Rimini orange 180 x 270 cm
5. Olive Yellow 180 x 270 cm

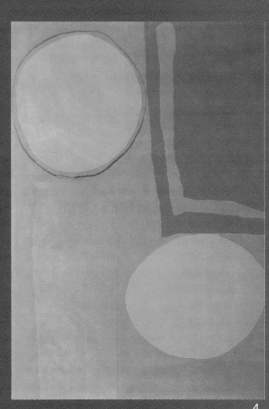

3

4

5

25 Store Street
South Crescent
London WC1E 7BL
t: +44(0) 20 7323 3300
email: questions@imagination.com
www.imagination.com

Imagination

"The range of Imagination's work stretches
conventional definitions of design" Stephen Bayley

"Imagination is an ideas company. If there's
a hierarchy, it's creativity before execution. That's
one of the reasons I enjoy going there – because
I feel stimulated creatively."
J Mays, Vice President, Design, Ford Motor Company

Imagination has worked with the world's leading
brands for over 25 years to become a global agency
with offices in London, New York, Detroit, Hong Kong,
Tokyo and Stockholm. It has a culture as distinctive as
its name. The quality of its people, the integrity of its
thought and its uncompromising commitment to
creativity, ultimately defines its approach.

Imagination pioneered the idea of brand experience.
That is, not just what a brand communicates in two
dimensions, but the emotions, feelings and responses
it can arouse in all dimensions. It has achieved this
through its unique multi-disciplinary offer, employing
architects, interior designers, graphic designers,
writers, film makers, photographers, lighting and
multimedia experts, all under one roof.

By orchestrating architectural and environmental
design, film, sound and lighting, Imagination creates
unique and immersive environmental experiences. The
sheer flexibility of Imagination's resource allows it to
work on any scale of environmental project, from those
environments that express the essence of a story, to
those which expand it to spectacular proportions.

See also volume Branding, Graphic and
New Media Design p. 38 and p. 116

1-3. Part of the lighting sequence to mark the launch of Tate
Modern.
4-5. Installation at London's Design Museum created
to temporarily house the 021C concept car designed by
Marc Newson.
6. GT40 exhibit at the Detroit Auto Show 2002.
7. Launch platform for Mazda's new global identity, Detroit
2002.
8. Mercury environment at the Detroit Auto Show 2002.
9. Land Rover exhibit at the Detroit Auto Show 2002.
10. Guinness transport story at Guinness Storehouse, Dublin.
11. 'Gravity' event at the Guinness Storehouse launch.
12-13. Schiphol Airport Interior by Virgile and Stone Associates
Ltd, a subsidiary company of The Imagination Group.

1

2

3

4

5

6

7

8

9

10

11

12

13

JudgeGiLL Design Consultancy

Management: Kevin Gill
Contacts: Lindsey Blythe
Staff: 12
Founded: 1993
Memberships: Design Business Association

3 Cobourg Street
Manchester M1 3GY
t: +44 (0) 161 228 3066/f: +44 (0) 161 228 0137
email: info@judgegill.co.uk
www.judgegill.co.uk

JudgeGill are a design consultancy providing fresh, progressive design, creating unique solutions for the retail, leisure and commercial sectors.
Our competencies include spatial design, graphics branding and project implementation

From your initial idea, our process explores project context, matching team skills to key design stages. In our relationships with clients, consultants and manufacturers, collaboration is essential.

Sharing knowledge and ideas encourages participation and enjoyment, whilst maintaining a sense of humour. We believe creativity isn't measured by budget.

Clients
JD Sports Plc
French Connection
Adidas
Ted Baker
New Look
size?
Virgin
Homes4u

See also volume Branding, Graphic and New Media Design p. 42

01. Ted Baker, Bluewater.
A fifty tonne installation with steel frames, toughened glass panelling and local stone.
02. Cobra, London.
Cobra is synonymous with the fashion concious culture.
03. Object Gallery, Manchester.
An independent urban art boutique.
04. size?, Selfridges London.
Layering of graphic material and footwear product in a constantly fresh and stimulating environment.
05. JudgeGill promtional T-shirt,
The 'JudgeGill team' with humourous washing instructions.
06. Ted Baker, Bluewater.

JudgeGill
Interiors
Graphics

Project ref.
240-AB-0898
Image 01

Project ref.
342-AB-0800
Image 02

Project ref.
344-AB-0301
Image 03

Jump
multi-disciplinary
design studio

Management: Simon Jordan, Shaun Fernandes
Contacts: Simon Jordan
Staff: 10
Founded: 2001

35 Britannia Row
UK
London N1 8QH
t: +44 (0)20 7688 0080
email: simon@jump-studios.com
www.jump-studios.com

Formed in 2001 Jump is a design and architectural studio that believes real design innovation comes from breaking down barriers between creative disciplines. The studio is built on a diverse mix of cultural and creative talent, fuelling an approach that thinks beyond routinely applied solutions.

Based in London and a recently established satellite office in Italy, Jump reaches beyond the core team to collaborate with international innovators from fashion, art, anthropology and the academic world in an ongoing quest to challenge expectations and redefine boundaries.

This has led to a broad spectrum of projects tackled including architectural, product, packaging and graphic design. Jump's work has been acclaimed internationally in publications including Domus, Ottagono, Design Report, Wired, Abitare, Blueprint, Time Out, GQ, Frame, The New York Times, The Guardian, ID, Creative Review and The Financial Times.

1. CAN vending bar
2. Barbershop retail concept for Unilever
3. Installation for Levi's premium ranges at Pitti Immagine, Florence
4. Alan Journo boutique, Via Condotti, Rome
5. Alan Journo boutique, Via Condotti, Rome
6. Naming, identity and structural packaging for Puur ice cream
7. Bacardi Breezer bar at Space nightclub, Ibiza

3

4

5

6

7

Oakwood dc
Stategic integrated design

Management: Phil Marshall / Neil Sims / Chris Jones
Contacts: Phil Marshall / Chris Jones
Staff: 42
Founded: 1995
Memberships: British Design Initiative / Institute of Directors

7 Park Street
Bristol BS1 5NF
t: +44 (0)11 7983 6789/f: +44 (0)11 7983 7323
email: user@oakwood-dc.com
www.oakwood-dc.com

Company profile

Oakwood dc was founded by three partners who shared the vision of ensuring their clients' commercial success by consistently delivering creative and impactful design, combined with a high quality cost service. From this beginning in 1995, Oakwood dc has grown into a strategic design consultancy that spans three inter-related disciplines:

Oakwood sd specialises in strategic graphic design from corporate identity, branding and literature through to packaging and direct mail. Oakwood 3d concentrates on designing and building the structures that make up creative retail and leisure environments, while Oakwood idc works exclusively with screen-based media to create dynamic websites, database-driven applications, CD-Rom presentations and interactive animations.

The strength of Oakwood dc is its team of individual characters and personalities, with diverse backgrounds and experiences. Our talented team works hand-in-hand with company professionals from various industries to ensure that the commercial relationship between the product or brand and the creative design is guaranteed.

See also volume Branding, Graphic and New Media Design p. 52 and p. 118

1. Concept and design for new carrier operations exhibit at the Fleet Air Arm Museum, Yeovilton. Completion in August 2002.

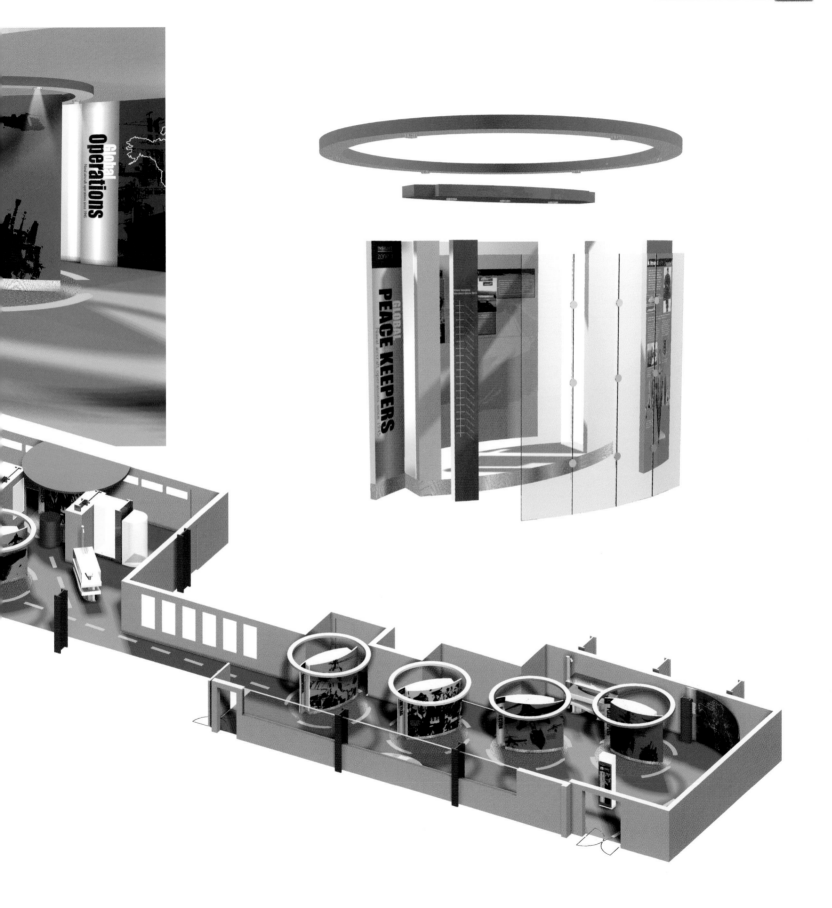

Management: tom redpath; jon muskett
Contacts: tom redpath
Staff: 10
Founded: 1996

7 Tilney Court
London EC1V 9BQ
t: +44 (0)20 7253 9005/f: +44 (0)20 7253 9004
email: studio@pathdesign.co.uk
www.pathdesign.co.uk

Path Design specialise in retail interiors, providing
well considered, commercially effective and innovative
solutions to their clients' requirements. Their involve-
ment in retail projects cover all aspects of store design
including branded environments, space planning,
visual merchandising, signage, merchandise equipment, documentation and project management.

Path's client list includes many high street brands
with whom they pride themselves on the longevity of
their relationships.

1. Malcolm Betts
2. Malcolm Betts
3. Coast
4. Coast
5. Virgin
6. Kookaï
7. Oasis
8. Oasis

Paul Daly Design Studio Ltd
Branding, Spatial design, Furniture & Product Design

Management: *Paul Daly*
Contacts: *Anna Hernestal*
Staff: *10*
Founded: *1987*

11 Hoxton Square
London N1 6NU
t: +44 (0)20 7613 4855/f: +44 (0)20 7613 5848
email: studio@pauldaly.com
www.pauldaly.com

Company profile

Paul Daly Design Studio is an award winning, multi-disciplinary company, based in London's expanding urban creative centre, Hoxton Square. The Studio has designed and branded numerous works, ranging from products and furniture through to residential interiors, commercial spaces, graphics and corporate identity.

The cohabitation of the design and manufacturing processes encourages the dialogue between traditional and contemporary materials. This is central to the Studio's design philosophy.

The Studio exhibits regularly at "100% Design", London, "Salone del Mobile", Milan and Tokyo designweek, Japan.

Client list

AP Hartley Buildings Ltd (Jam Factory), UK
The Breakfast Group, UK
Borodino Ltd, Bermuda
Champion Sports, Ireland
Chivas Regal, UK
Coca Cola
The Elbow Room Management Company Plc, UK
Exposure Promotions Ltd, UK
E & Y, Japan
Lab Ltd, U.K
Lee Chapman - Teatro, London, UK
Love Boat Ltd, UK
Maxray Inc, Japan
Merrill Lynch, UK
Nude Ltd, Ireland
Ozwald Boateng Ltd, UK
Radius Interiors Ltd, UK
Rizla Rolling Paper, UK
The Seagram Spirits and Wine Group, UK
Six Continents Retail Ltd, UK
Ultimate Leisure Group plc, UK
U2 (rock group), Worldwide

1. Elbow Room, London 2. Time, Newcastle 3. Logo & brand identity 4. Love, Oxford 5. Ozwald Boateng showroom, London 6. Logo & brand identity 7. Love, Oxford 8. Cut, Newcastle 9. Logo & brand identity 10. Loop, Bridlington 11. Nude, Dublin, Ireland 12. Time, Newcastle 13. The Sea, Newcastle 14. Logo & brand identity 15. Barbican Apartment, London 16. HCYJLMS stools, Japan 17. Chase, Newcastle

[10]

[13]

[14]

The Elbow Room ®

[11]

[15]

[16]

[12]

[17]

Powell-Tuck
Associates
Architecture and
Design

Management: Julian Powell-Tuck, Angus Shepherd
Contacts: Julian Powell-Tuck
Staff: 16
Founded: 1990
Memberships: FRSA, RIBA, CSD

6 Stamford Brook Road
London W6 0XH
t: +44 (0)20 8749 7700/f: +44 (0)20 8749 8737
email: jpowelltuck@powelltuck.co.uk
www.powelltuck.co.uk

Powell-Tuck Associates is a multi-disciplinary architecture and design practice employing one environmental
designer, seven architects, five interior designers and
three product designers. We specialise in the fitting
out, alteration and extension of existing buildings,
many of which are listed.

Clients come to us when they want an individual and
unique design solution combining architectural
alterations and interior fit out. Whilst creative,
our work also responds to the way a building is to be
occupied and used. Commissions vary in scale from
master-planning and development strategies to
furniture design and signage.

Previous work includes the projects listed here. But
we prefer not to be pigeonholed, and accept work
whatever the level of design co-ordination involved.

Creative office space
Presentation spaces
Corporate entertainment and catering facilities
Art /music venues
Recording studios
Post production studios
TV studios
Museum and exhibition spaces
Healthcare /surgeries
Specialist retail /hair salons
Showrooms
Specialist·work spaces
Sports facilities
Dealing rooms
Houses for private clients
Specialist product and furniture design
Specialist signage design

1

2

3

1-13. Bloomberg London Headquarters
Bloomberg LP
2001 - 2002

4

5

7

6

8

9

10

11

12

13

Rawfish Design Consultants

Management: Andy Barlow
Contacts: Andy Barlow
Staff: 5
Founded: 1993

54 Chapel Street
Manchester M3 7AA
t: +44 (0)161 839 7680/f: +44 (0)161 833 9515
email: design@raw-fish.demon.co.uk
www.rawfishdesign.co.uk

Profile

Rawfish Design Consultants was established in 1993
with the intention of adding value and creativity
with appropriateness of application to all areas of
commercial interior design. Rawfish's work is of
a contemporary nature and there is a strong belief
in not creating pastiches of the past, with this at the
forefront of their thinking Rawfish strive to create
innovative and inventive solutions to their clients'
design problems and as a result have a high success
rate with repeat business.

Rawfish Design Consultants are architects, interior
designers and graphic designers and as such create
a multidisciplinary team focused on advancing creative,
commercially aware thinking in sectors which include
retail, leisure, office and public domains. Whether it be
new build apartment blocks around the UK or the roll
out of Haagen Dazs Cafés throughout the UK and
Ireland Rawfish offer the same level of service and
commitment to creating buildings and spaces which
reflect their attitude to design.

Recent clients include

Bolo Menswear
Choice Design Wear
Dream Loft Co
Dynamic Earth Enterprizes
Ellis Brigham Sports
Giancarlo Ricci
Global Travel
Haagen Dazs Cafés
LBS Recording Studios
MC Group
The Museum on Science & Industry in Manchester
Reebok UK
Tessuti Quality Clothing
Tilfen
Torres & Partners
Vinyl Exchange Records
Whitbread plc
WOW Developments
Yates and Suddell opticians
Zest

Entrance, ticketing and retail at The Museum of Science and Industry in Manchester

Opposite page from left to right, by row:

The Museum of Science & Industry in Manchester The Museum of Science & Industry in Manchester
Choice Design Wear, Bluewater Choice Design Wear, Romford
Our Dynamic Earth, Edinburgh Bolo, Hull

Choice Design Wear, Romford Choice Design Wear (Women), Lakeside
Tessuti, Chester Zest Café, Manchester
The Museum of Science & Industry in Manchester Choice Design Wear (Men), Lakeside

LBS Recording Studio, Manchester
Torres & Partners, Manchester
Paco Restaurant, Manchester

Rawfish Design Consultants

Redjacket

Management: Martyn Bullock
Contacts: Dan Higgott
Staff: 15
Founded: 1990

38-40 Glasshill Street
London SE1 0QR
t: +44 (0)20 7928 4466/f: +44 (0)20 7928 4477
email: info@redjacketdesign.com
www.redjacketdesign.com

3D Brand Specialists

Redjacket's aim has always been to bridge the gap between the overtly commercial end of interior design world and highly creative small start-up companies who consistently produce thought-provoking work, but historically stood little chance of working with international brands. Having identified the need, Redjacket was founded in May 1990.

To this day creativity remains high on our list of priorities without losing sight of the commercial realities of the projects we contribute to. Over a decade on, we are now a multidisciplinary consultancy with completed projects now operating as far afield as China and Australia.

Our aim is to combine our track record within Interior and Graphic design with Interactive technology, developing responsive environments which react to people, engaging and entertaining our clients' customers.

1. Costa Coffee
2. B.A.T. China
3. Six Continents Retail
4. Virgin Megastores
5. Costa Coffee
6. South West Trains
7. Daminis
8. Regina Rubens/LVMH
9. Revlon International
10. Jones Knowles Ritchie

www.redjacketdesign.com

Shopkit Designs Limited Shopkit Designs Limited / Shopkit Export Limited

Contacts: Barry Blandford, Pritpal Matharu, Paul McCarthy
Founded: 1980

100 Cecil Street
Watford
Hertfordshire WD24 5AD
t: +44 (0)1923 818282/f: +44 (0)1923 818280
email: sales@shopkit.com
www.shopkit.com

Shopkit GmbH:
Oststr. 36
40211 Dusseldorf
Germany
t: +49 (0) 211/ 38 69 6-0/f: +49 (0) 211/ 38 69 6-24
email: info@shopkit.de
www.shopkit.de

Company Profile

Shopkit Designs are experienced in all types of interiors including shops, offices, banks, restaurants, window displays and exhibitions, offering clients a complete design and build service, from the initial concept/ planning stages, through manufacture and on to complete installation.

Included in the products and services provided by Shopkit is the most comprehensive range of display equipment, low-voltage lighting and cable and rod suspension systems available today.

Continuing to expand worldwide, Shopkit now has offices in the USA, Europe, the Middle East and Far East, with products produced locally as well as in the UK.

Client List

Arthur Anderson Consulting
Apple
BBC
BMW a.G.
BP Plc
British Airways Travel Shops
British Telecom
GSK Glaxo Smith Kline
Harrods
Hasbro
HDI Versicherung a.G.
Hitachi Data Systems Limited
IBM UK Limited
The London Stock Exchange
JP Morgan Chase Bank
Nortel Networks plc
Portugal Telecom
Renault UK Limited
Charles Schwab Europe
Selfridges & Co
Shell UK Exploration
Sony
Sparkasse

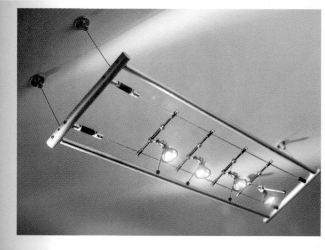

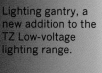

Lighting gantry, a new addition to the TZ Low-voltage lighting range.

Backlit Peg Wall system with low-voltage lighting, designed for Ports International, Beijing.

Cable suspended cabinet, part of Shopkit's Cable and Rod display system.

Three tiered bar and counter, with slide out display shelf.

Stainless steel rod display and signage system, part of the Signkit range.

Internet Cafe, part of the Sytner BMW showroom, The City, Central London.

Custom made cabinets and retail environment, including an internet cafe, Sytner BMW Showroom, City of London.

Studio Hagger

Management: James Hagger, Kate Killeen
Contacts: Kate Killeen
Staff: 10
Founded 1996

104-106 Chiswick High Road
London W4 1PU
t: +44 (0)20 8747 3000/f: +44 (0)20 8747 1444/m:
+44 (0)777 584 6699
email: katek@studiohagger.com
www.studiohagger.com

Studio Hagger is a company dedicated to the Brand Experience.
Our design is based upon getting right to the heart of brand - be it retail, corporate or product - and then expressing that heart through every part of the customer journey. More than that, we seek always to do this in a way that engages - and charms.

The 3D face of a brand is a potent part of its communication - perhaps the most potent. Bland, smart boxes or me-too solutions just can't exploit this potency. Big, brand-ownable ideas, beautifully executed can. We can.

Our offer extends from brand concept and positioning to naming, brand and sub brand identity, retail and environment design and project management.

client list
ACM (Academy of Contemporary Music)
BAA,
Bank of Ireland
Claritas Europe
Dyno
Eagle Star
Fleetwood
Land Rover
LEGO
Marks & Spencer
New Look
SAS Euroshop
The Savile Row Company
Ten Nailbar
Vinopolis, City of Wine
World Duty Free

1. The retail finale to a two-acre wine experience in the City of London: Vinopolis, City of Wine
2. A retail brand experience created to bring this former shirt manufacturer to this famous street: 40 Savile Row
3. Bespoke furniture designs to echo the bespoke tailoring offer - and to entertain and charm the consumer: 40 Savile Row
3. One of Europe's largest duty-free shops - planned for total flexibility according to passenger flow: World Duty Free Europe
4. One of Europe's largest duty-free shops planned for total flexibility according to passenger flow: World Duty Free, Manchester Airport
5. Showcasing premium fragrance and cosmetics brands in a strongly branded retail envelope: World Duty Free, Heathrow, Terminal 3
6-9. A branded nail bar - from identity and retail environment design to sub brand, promotional and advertising design: TEN

Two by Two consultants Ltd
Retail, Exhibition and Interior Design

Management: Salvatore Cicero, Ashwin Shaw
Contacts: Salvatore Cicero, Ashwin Shaw
Staff: 12
Founded: 1995

Britannia Walk
151-157 City Road
London EC1V 1JH
t: +44 (0)20 7253 0081/f: +44 (0)20 7253 0091
email: zebra@twobytwo.co.uk
www.twobytwo.co.uk

Company profile

Two by Two is a small company with big ideas.
We approach every project, big or small, with the
same degree of enthusiasm, imagination and care.
We believe in the power of creativity and the craft of
implementation. The close working relationship we
build with our clients ensures a unique and relevant
outcome time after time. Salvatore Cicero and Ashwin
Shaw are the creative directors, and they offer the
benefit of many years' experience in Retail, Exhibition
and Interior design for a wide range of clients.

Clients include:

Budweiser
Coca-Cola
Colorcom
Corsini Consulting
Couture Brands
Dudley plc
Elemis London Ltd
Hi-Tec
Royal Mint
J Sainsbury plc
Satyajit Ray Foundation
Spofforths
Suzuki
The Wine Society
Tyndale Group
Vichy

This innovative spa provides a relaxing sanctuary, to
balance mind and body and restore harmony after the
stresses of everyday life. And it was Two by Two's task
to create the complete experience.

The starting point was the name and 'In harmony'
encapsulated all the right qualities. The visual identity
is a simple and stylish rendition of 'In', interlaced with
evocative subtext and harmonious shapes.

The characteristic elements of Japanese simplicity,
spirituality and hospitality are seamlessly interwoven
with Western modernity to create a new concept in Spa
environments - East meets West.

The interior is designed to be calming with natural
colours, fluid lines and subtle lighting. The relaxation
area is inspired by Japanese gardens with plants,
flowing water, aromatic candles and soft music.

Japanese tea and fresh fruit are an integral part of the
experience, reflecting Two by Two's brand promise for
'In Harmony' - excellence through attention to detail
every step of the way.

See also volume Product and Packaging Design p. 58

Warner Associates Corporate Interiors

Management: Ken Warner, Malcolm Harris & Paul Goodchild
Contacts: Ken Warner
Staff: 3
Founded: 1993

20 Upper Maudlin St
Bristol BS2 8DJ
t: 0117 9292011/f: 0117 9297094
email: info@warner-associates.co.uk
www.warner-associates.co.uk

Company Profile

Founded in 1993, Warner Associates are award-winning Corporate Interiors experts providing high quality office Design & Build services to national and international companies.

Our business is to improve your business.

Our Services

Analysis & Project Feasibilities
Building Surveys and CAD Plans
Block & Space Planning
Concept Design and Specifications
Detail Interior Design of specialist areas
IT Services Design
Building Services Design
Project Management
Office Fitout
Furniture supply
Internal and external relocations
Compliance to regulations

Selected Clients

Albert Goodman
Arjo Wiggins
Arno Fords
BBM Carlson
Brann
Cuprinol
Dun & Bradstreet
Ernst & Young
Grant Thornton
Iambic Productions
Helphire
Jelf Insurance
Jersey Energy
Kneehigh Theatre
Learning & Skills Council
National Power
PeopleSoft
Profund
Securicor
Soil Association
Telia
Tentendigital
TLT Solicitors
Triodos Bank
Woodspring District Council

WARNER
ASSOCIATES

CORPORATE INTERIORS

Zynk Design Consultants

Management: Clinton Pritchard, Stavros Theodoulou
Staff: 4

10 The Chandlery
50 Westminster Bridge Road
London SE1 7QY
t: +44 (0)20 7721 7444/f: +44 (0)20 7721 7443
email: info@zynkdesign.com
www.zynkdesign.com

Zynk design consultants were formed in the spring of
1998 by Clinton Pritchard and Stavros Theodoulou,
managing partners. With extensive experience in the
retail, corporate, hospitality and health and fitness
market sectors, we offer an extended level of interior
and graphic design consultancy services, focusing on
the development of branded environments.

From initial concept to project completion, all clients
are assigned a managing partner responsible for the
delivery of the clients objectives. Often these are
unclear or unknown at the outset and using our skills
and experience as commercial branding designers, we
initiate a dialogue that allows us to get 'under the skin'
of an organisation, or operation and assess the
strategic needs and commercial objectives that are
desired or required.

Our experience has led us to best describe our
complimentary skills as those of 'Brand Evolutionists'.

*See also volume Branding, Graphic and
New Media Design p. 106*

*AVANTI - Birmingham University
Campus - Campus
CLIENT: BIRMINGHAM
UNIVERSITY
PROJECT: Brand Identity,
Environmental Graphics, Signage,
Interior Design, Implementation.*

INTERNAL SIGNAGE / SERVERY COUNTER HEADERS

*GO - Birmingham University
Campus - Café
CLIENT: BIRMINGHAM
UNIVERSITY
PROJECT: Brand Identity,
Environmental Graphics, Signage,
Interior Design, Implementation.*

*LIME - Bar & Restaurant
CLIENT: LIME ENTERTAINMENTS
LTD.
PROJECT: Brand Identity,
Environmental Graphics, Menu's,
Marketing Literature,
Interior Design, Implementation.*

LITERATURE - CORPORATE BROCHURE

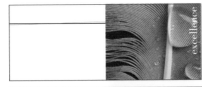

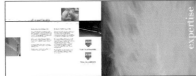

club indigo
fitness | health | life

feel INDIGOod

get INDIGo'EC

DIRECT MAIL - POSTCARDS

brand evolutionists...
zynk Zn

isospa
Fitness Health

Workout • Relax • You choose

LITERATURE - TIMETABLES

STATIONERY

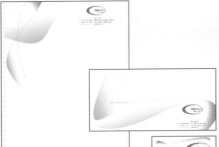

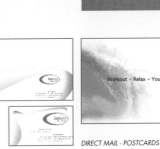

DIRECT MAIL - POSTCARDS

Advertisements

BIS BIS BIS

MAGAZINESMAGAZINE
BOOKSBOOKS

BIS Publishers, Amsterdam
BIS Publishers, Amsterdam

YOUTH CULTURE DUTCH DESIG
MAGAZINESMAGAZINE
BOOKSBOOKS

BIS Publishers, Amsterdam
BIS Publishers, Amsterdam

BIS

Amsterdam

MAGAZINES
BOOKS

GRAPHIC DESIGN
WEBSITE GRAPHICS INTERACTION DESIGN TYPOGRAPHY
MAGAZINESMAGAZINESMAGAZINES
BOOKSBOOKSBOOKS
VISUAL COMMUNICATION
INTERIORINTERIOR

BIS Publishers, Amsterdam   BIS Publishers, Amsterdam   BIS Publishers, Amsterdam

ARCHITECTUREARCHITECTURE
MAGAZINESMAGAZINES
BOOKSBOOKS

BIS Publishers, Amsterdam   BIS Publishers, Amsterdam

ENTER

www.bispublishers.nl

exhibits international

- concept design
- design engineering
- project management
- logistics
- production

Management (Europe): Louk de Sévaux
Contacts: Norbert Wilmering
Staff: 25

European office:
Plotterstraat 1
1033 RX Amsterdam
The Netherlands
T: +31 20 581 3030
F: +31 20 581 3031
Email: norbertw@exhibits-intl.com
www.exhibitsinternational.com

Head office:
431 Horner Avenue
Toronto, Ontario
Canada M8W 4W3
T: +1 416 252 2818
F: +1 416 252 3708

Focusing upon clear cut communication with
our clients and their appointed communication
consultancies or concept studios, we translate
key messages ranging from corporate identity,
campaigns in print, on-line and new media
into 3 dimensional environments.
Exhibits International excels in the creation of
3D environments which underwrite the corporate
message and expertise of an organization to
their target group.
From our Amsterdam and Toronto offices, we
provide global services on a turn key basis or
at any level throughout the creative or
implementation process. We preserve the message
and brand consistency in marketing
and communication projects such as

- exhibitions and displays
- museums
- trade shows
- interior and retail environments
- special brand related experience events
- sales meetings and conventions
- hospitality events

1. Nikepark 1998, Paris
2. Royal Weddings, De Nieuwe Kerk, Amsterdam
3. Nike European Headquarters, Hilversum
3. Versatel 2000, Brussels
5. Nikepark 2000, Amsterdam
6. Niketown London
7. Unilever IBCC, Schiphol - Amsterdam

3

6

7

British Design Initiative

the focal point of british design

CORPORATE REGISTRATION   DESIGN INDUSTRY SURVEY   DESIGN NEWS SERVICE   DESIGN HANDBOOK 2003   DESIGN EXPORTS   DESIGN DIRECTORY   DESIGN ADVISORY SERVICE   DESIGN EVENTS

The British Design Initiative is an internationally recognised agency that provides a focal point for British design.

Established since 1993, it has built strong and trusted relationships with the UK's leading design agencies and with official design bodies, government and key media. Increasingly the British Design Initiative is working with those brand owners who strategically seek to align themselves with the design profession or provide products and services to the professions.

The BDI owns an accurate database of UK design agencies; design media, design awards and professional design bodies internationally. It currently has direct access to an estimated 85% of the entire UK market.

http://www.britishdesign.co.uk

British Design
2004
Call for entries

The next edition of this multi-volume survey of British design is scheduled for publication late 2003. It will provide the most comprehensive profile of design ever in this country, offering clients in the UK and abroad an essential guide to design services in Britain.

Make sure you're part of it!

If you are a designer or design agencies located in the UK and if you are interested in being included with a showcase profile in the next edition, please contact us. Do it today: the sooner you sign up, the more time you will have to create your entry.

Contact Marijke Wervers at BIS Publishers for information on how to submit your work, closure dates and conditions.

Marijke can be reached at: marijke@bispublishers.nl.
You can also find entry details on our website www.bispublishers.nl

51% Studios
1-5 Clerkenwell Road
London EC1M 5PA
United Kingdom

ACQ Architects
26 Mortimer Street
London W1N 7RA
United Kingdom

AD Creative Consultants
Royal Victoria Patriotic
Building
Studio 17/18
Trinity Road
London SW18 3SX
United Kingdom

BDP Design
16 Gresse Street
London W1A 4WD
United Kingdom

Blair Exhibition Design
12 St. James's Square
London SW1Y 4RB
United Kingdom

Carte Blanche
4-5 Fizroy Mews
London W1T 6DG
United Kingdom

Caulder Moore
The Coach House
273-a Sandycombe Road
Kew
London TW9 3LU
United Kingdom

Checkland Kindleysides
Charnwood Edge
Cossington
Leicester LE7 4UZ
United Kingdom

**Communication by
Design Ltd**
6 The Courthouse
38 Kingsland Road
London E2 8DD
United Kingdom

Conran Design Group
90/98 Goswell Road
London EC1V 7DF
United Kingdom

Corporate Edge
130 Hammersmith Road
London W14 0QL
United Kingdom

Corsie Naysmith I.D.C.
Threeways House
40-44 Clipstone Street
London W1P 7EA
United Kingdom

Dalziel & Pow
Design Consultants
5-8 Hardwick Street
London EC1R 4RG
United Kingdom

Design LSM
The Bath House
58 Livingstone Road
East Sussex
Hove BN3 3WL
United Kingdom

DJPA Partnership
Unit i4
22-24 Torrington Place
London WC1E 7HF
United Kingdom

Fern Green
www.ferngreen.com
studio@ferngreen.com

**Furneaux Stewart Design
& Communications**
16-E Portland Road
London W11 4LA
United Kingdom

Helen Yardley
A-Z Studios
3-5 Hardwidge Street
Bermondsey
London SE1 3SY
United Kingdom

Imagination Ltd
25 Store Street
South Cresent
London WC1E 7BL
United Kingdom

**JudgeGill Design
Consultancy**
3 Cobourg Street
Manchester M1 3GY
United Kingdom

Jump
35 Brittannia Row
London N1 8QH
United Kingdom

Oakwood dc
7 Park Street
Bristol BS1 5NF
United Kingdom

Path Design
7 Tilney Court
London EC1V 9BQ
United Kingdom

**Paul Daly Design
Studio Ltd.**
11 Hoxton Square
London N1 6NU
United Kingdom

Powell-Tuck Associates
6 Stamford Brook Road
London W6 0HX
United Kingdom

**Rawfish Design
Consultants**
54 Chapel Street
Manchester M3 7AA
United Kingdom

Redjacket
38-40 Glasshill Street
London SE1 0QR
United Kingdom

Shopkit Designs Ltd
100 Cecil Street
Watford
Hertfordshire WD24 5AD
United Kingdom

Studio Hagger
104-106 Chiswick High
Road
London W4 1PU
United Kingdom

Two by Two
Britannia Walk
151-157 City Road
London EC1V 1JH
United Kingdom

Warner Associates
20 Upper Maudlin Street
Bristol BS2 8DJ
United Kingdom

Zynk Design Consultants
10 The Chandlery
50 Westminster Bridge
Road
London SE1 7QY
United Kingdom

Publisher: BIS Publishers
Herengracht 370-372
1016 CH Amsterdam
The Netherlands
T +31 (0) 20 524 75 60
F +31 (0) 20 524 75 57
E bis@bispublishers.nl
www.bispublishers.nl

Production coordination:
BIS Publishers, Amsterdam:
Susanne Verhoog

Sales management:
BIS Publishers, Amsterdam:
Marijke Wervers

The British Design
Initiative Limited
2 Peterborough Mews
Parsons Green
London SW6 3BL
T +44 (0) 7384 3435
F +44 (0) 7371 5343
E info@britishdesign.co.uk
www.britishdesign.co.uk

Design: August, London

Cover photography: Richard Caldicott

Prelims photography: Nigel Shafran

Text revision: Tibbon Translations,
Amsterdam: Sam Herman

Layout: Backup grafisch vormgeven,
Amsterdam: Onno de Haan
Jos B Koene, Amsterdam

Database publishing:
Iticus, Amsterdam: Marco Kijlstra

Printing: TWA, Signapore

Acknowledgements: Laurent Benner,
Raphael Helfi, Maxine J Horn, Nigel
Jackson, Christine Losecaat, Alex Rich,
Mini Rich, David Spero, Rei Terau